THIS BOOK BELONGS TO

------------------------------------

For Douglas and Theo
– K.R.W

First edition published in 2022 by Flying Eye Books,
an imprint of Nobrow Ltd. 27 Westgate Street, London, E8 3RL.

Text © Kim Ryall Woolcock 2022
Illustrations © Stacey Thomas 2022

1 3 5 7 9 10 8 6 4 2

Published in the US by Nobrow (US) Inc.
Printed in Latvia on FSC® certified paper.

FSC
www.fsc.org

MIX
Paper from
responsible sources
FSC® C002795

ISBN: 978-1-838748-53-1

www.flyingeyebooks.com

Kim Ryall Woolcock            Stacey Thomas

# It's Tough to be Tiny

Flying Eye Books

# CONTENTS

# IT'S TOUGH TO BE TINY...

When you're tiny, some things feel out of reach.
Bigger creatures seem more powerful than you.
It's not easy to get noticed. And sometimes
you get squashed.

But there's tiny and then there's *tiny*.

*Tardigrades*, also known
as water bears, are smaller
than the dot above this "i".

When you're that tiny, there are a lot of bigger creatures that want to eat you.

*Wolf spider*

*Cricket*

What's it like to be so small? How do these tiny creatures stay safe, or hunt for their lunch? It helps to have a superpower. Like spring-loaded jumps, or microscopic toxic darts. Some tiny creatures have armor, or wear a scary costume. Some buddy up with a bigger creature (which is pretty nice for the bigger creatures, too).

# JUMP FOR YOUR LIFE!

When you're really tiny, your feet and legs are tiny, too. Tiny legs can't run very fast. A powerful jump can take you far away from predators much faster than the blink of an eye.

*Gears in a planthopper's legs*

## Interlocking Legs

These little fuzzbutts are baby **planthoppers.** They have a special trick tucked in their fluff: super-strong back legs that let them leap away. Their jumps are so powerful, they need a way to make sure both legs push off at precisely the same time. They use gears! The gears synchronize their legs so planthoppers can jump straight ahead. If one leg pushed sooner, the planthopper would go into a crazy spin. No other animal on Earth has legs like this.

*Songthrush*

3 mm

Although baby planthoppers are only a few millimeters long, about the size of a grain of rice, they can jump distances 100 times their own length. They could jump right out of this book!

## Look Ma, no legs!

**Springtails** jump away from predators without using their legs! They have a stiff tail called a furca that they bend around and clip to their bellies, like a seat belt for safety. Except this seat belt doesn't keep them in place—it flings them far away. When there's danger, they unclip their secret spring-loaded furca. It whips out and hits the ground, somersaulting them into the sky. They tumble when they land.

5 mm

Springtails can jump a few times before they need to rest and re-load their spring.

5

4

3

2

The springtail somersault sequence

# SHOOT THEM WITH TOXINS!

If you're slow, it might be better to stand your ground and fight a predator. Some slow creatures carry weapons. From toxic darts to bad smells to sprays of burning chemicals, there are lots of ways to say "don't eat me!"

## Sea slugs that sting

Most **nudibranchs** are smaller than a pencil sharpener (2 cm). With their soft bodies and colorful tufted backs, they don't seem deadly. But all those colors are like a neon sign saying "eat me if you dare." Many nudibranchs taste terrible, and some can sting with toxic darts. They steal their weapons from some of the deadliest creatures in the ocean, like stinging corals and anemones, while munching them for lunch. Nudibranch mouths are tough, and the stingers they're stealing don't hurt them. The nudibranch swallows the stingers, then stashes them in its colorful spikes. When a predator touches them, it gets squirted with toxic darts!

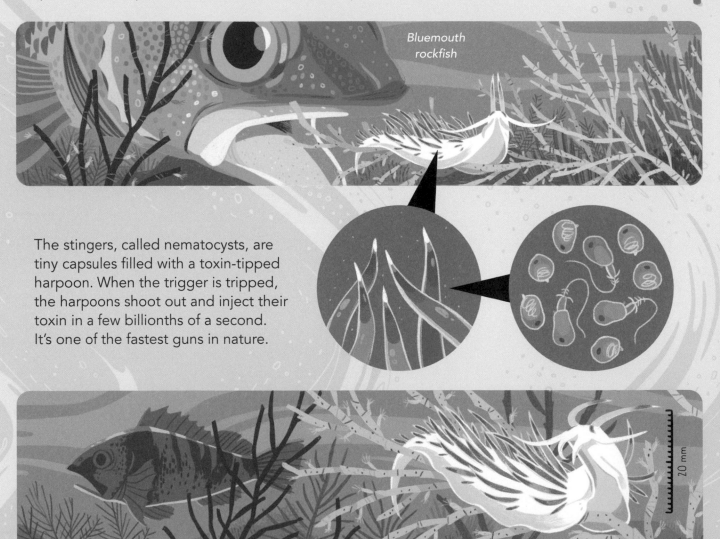

Bluemouth rockfish

The stingers, called nematocysts, are tiny capsules filled with a toxin-tipped harpoon. When the trigger is tripped, the harpoons shoot out and inject their toxin in a few billionths of a second. It's one of the fastest guns in nature.

20 mm

## If you can't sting, then stink!

**Millipedes** have so many legs (up to 1306!). You'd think all those legs would make them super speedy. But no, they're slow. Maybe it's hard to control so many legs at once. They stay safe by carrying chemical weapons. When threatened, they can curl into a spiral and squirt stinky or blistering chemicals out of special glands. For some species, the chemicals just ooze out—but others can shoot out jets of burning poison. Some can ooze enough of a poisonous gas called cyanide to kill small creatures like birds or mice.

*Bewick's wren*

Millipedes are the leggiest animals on earth. Thank goodness they don't wear shoes.

13

# WEAR ARMOR

Armor that is hard to bite through can stop predators that want to eat you. Some creatures build it out of materials they find, others grow it around their bodies.

10 mm

## Underwater armor

*Young caddisflies*, called larvae, have small, soft bodies. But they live in fast-flowing streams, where they might get tumbled into rocks, or swept away by the current. And the streams are full of fish that love to eat them. They build armored cases out of twig bits, leaf shreds, or grains of sand. They choose the pieces with care, and glue them together with stretchy silk that stays sticky, even underwater. When they find just the right piece, they coat it with silk, then stick it in place, like they are building a wall.

Caddisflies' cases do double duty. They provide both protection from predators' jaws and camouflage, like an armored sleeping bag sewn out of an invisibility cloak.

Night, night, sleep tight.
Don't let the big bad predators bite.

## Armored apartments

*Corals* are collections of tiny tentacled creatures that look like flowers. Each one is called a *polyp* and can be smaller than a grain of rice or a bit bigger than your baby toe (1 mm to 5 cm). Polyps pull elements out of the seawater to build hard homes around their soft bodies. They like to live together, so they build next to each other, like a lumpy apartment building. Different species build in different shapes: brains, pillars, plates, mounds, or branching trees.

Some coral reefs are 4,000 years old and are so big they can be seen from space.

The polyps live in their rocky shelters during the day, and poke their tentacles out at night to feed. The tentacles are armed with tiny toxic stingers, called nematocysts, that sting whatever they touch.

# ARMOR OF GLASS

Intricate like snowflakes, too small to see, busily spinning sunlight into sugar—these are **diatoms**.

Diatoms are a very simple type of aquatic plant called algae.

Everywhere there is water, there are diatoms. Diatoms are so tiny, between 10 and 100 could fit, side by side, in a drop of water.

They are tiny and delicate, but they wear armor, too. They build their beautiful shells of glass. The two halves fit together like a jewel box. Some look like snowflakes, sea stars, or even alien space ships.

Their glass houses help keep them safe.

# WEAR A DISGUISE

Instead of being afraid of predators, why not make them afraid of you? Some small creatures wear a scary costume. Others wear camouflage so it's hard for predators to see them.

## I'm a snake, not a snack!

Even not-so-small creatures, like caterpillars, need protection from the birds that want to eat them. **Spicebush swallowtail caterpillars** wear a creepy costume to keep predators away. It's like they are dressed up as the predators of their predators. Just behind their real head, they have two fake eyespots. Curled up inside a leaf shelter, they look more like a snake than a snack. Anyone peeking around in the leaves to eat them would get a fright!

If the caterpillars' disguise doesn't work, they have something special, called an osmeterium, hidden just behind their head. When they stick it out, it looks like a snake's forked tongue! The forked tongue oozes a super-stinky chemical that they try to "lick" onto whatever is trying to eat them.

## The brighter the better

The **Asian jewel beetle** hides with beauty. Its body shimmers, reflecting many colors that change with the light.

They are so bright—are they really hiding? It seems like a terrible idea for a small insect to wear a glittery rainbow shell. But the sparkly sheen helps these beetles hide in shiny green leaves. The shifting colors act like the different blocks of color in "camo" fabric, making it harder to spot the outline of the beetle.

Sometimes the best disguise is…glitter!

# GO FOR GROSS

Who goes looking for their lunch in a pile of poop?
Most creatures don't! Looking like something no one
would ever want to eat can be an excellent way to hide.

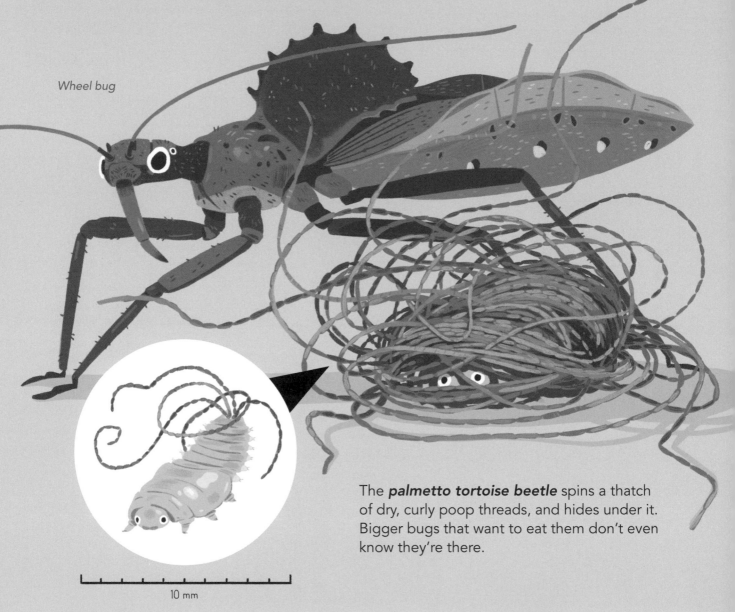

*Wheel bug*

10 mm

The **palmetto tortoise beetle** spins a thatch
of dry, curly poop threads, and hides under it.
Bigger bugs that want to eat them don't even
know they're there.

Larvae of the **horse mint tortoise beetle** carry
a poop umbrella with their butt. To make it extra
yucky, they fill it with toxic chemicals from the plants
they eat. They can lift it up, wave it around, or even
swing it like a club. Bigger bugs consider the poop
shield to be toxic waste, and just stay away.

# And if you do get eaten?

If you're a **water scavenger beetle**, you walk right out the back door. Just round black dots, these beetles don't look all that special. But they are actually escape artists.

They're so small, a frog can down one in a single gulp. You'd think that would be the end of them.

Black spotted frog

But no, if they find themselves inside a frog, they just use their legs and escape the frog's innards.

It would normally take more than a day for the frog to digest its dinner. But these beetles escape in a few minutes.

5 mm

When they get to the back door (the frog's butt), the frog poops them out.

# TINY HUNTERS

Super-small creatures that don't like to eat vegetables have to hunt
if they want to eat. But how do carnivores the size of a speck of dust
go hunting? They might carry special weapons to hunt creatures
bigger than they are. They might vacuum up smaller creatures as
they swim by. Or they might fool their prey by looking harmless.
Very powerful jaws might come in handy. Some can skate on water,
or build secret forts so they can jump out when dinner walks by.

**Peacock spiders** are tiny and
fuzzy, but they hunt like tigers
do, by pouncing on their prey.

Fruit fly

Male peacock spiders are also fabulous dancers. They do elaborate mating dances to win over female spiders.

23

# THROW THINGS AT 'EM

If you're tiny, having a special weapon can help you to hunt your lunch. Secret weapons might even help you catch creatures faster than you are!

*Tiger blenny*

Some cone snails eat worms or even other snails.

## Slow but fast

Snails are SO slow. They hardly seem like good hunters. But tiny **cone snails**, with their pretty patterned shells, are some of the fastest guns in the sea. They hunt fast-swimming fish as big as they are. And then they swallow them whole. Hidden under their beautiful shells, inside a tube that looks like an elephant's trunk, they keep a secret weapon: a harpoon tooth. They can shoot this tooth into their prey in just a few microseconds. When it hits the prey, the harpoon tooth injects powerful venom. The snail hauls the prey in, hooked on the tooth, like reeling in a fish caught on a hook. Then it wraps the fish up in its stretchy sack-like lips (called a rostrum), and digests it.

## Goo gun

**Velvet worms** have soft bodies that are full of liquid, like walking water balloons. They don't have a hard shell, or even any bones. But they are deadly hunters. They sneak up on their prey at night, and shoot them with sticky goo, using two nozzles on their face. The goo nozzles wiggle back and forth, like a garden hose at full blast that no one's holding on to. The goo splatters everywhere, and then hardens into a cage of tough threads, trapping the prey.

The struggling prey makes the goo harden into stiff threads by stretching it, similar to how kneading transforms bread from a sticky lump into a stretchy dough.

Termite

Once the prey is trapped, the velvet worm bites it to inject innard-melting enzymes, then drinks the prey milkshake.

# BRING IT . . .

Some creatures sit and wait for their food to come to them. It's like getting a food delivery!

## Tiny trumpet with a tractor beam

**Stentor** are so small, they can live in a drop of water. They are invisible unless you have a microscope. The rim of the trumpet is lined with tiny hairs that wave to create a current that sweeps any nearby creatures straight into the stentor's mouth, like when you pull the plug in the sink and water swirls down the drain.

To find a good hunting ground, stentor ball themselves up like a sock, then swim around. When they find somewhere they like, they grab on with their holdfast and stretch out into their hunting trumpet shape and start up the tractor beam, which drags nearby creatures into their body to be digested.

Stentor can stretch to 5–10 times their normal length.

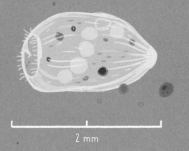

2 mm

## Wave those toxic tentacles

Tiny hunters called *hydra* live in water droplets too. They look like tubes with tentacles on top—and the tentacles are loaded with toxins. The tentacles are covered with nematocysts, spring-loaded stingers that are triggered by a touch. They shoot out in a few billionths of a second, paralyze the prey, and the hydra stuffs it inside its sock-like body for digestion. They are so stretchy, they can eat prey bigger than themselves.

Copepod

20 mm

Hydra are incredibly tough. Cut one in half, and you will get two hydra. Turn one inside out and it will just flip itself right side round again. Put one in the blender … and the cells will rearrange into a living hydra.

# LOOK HARMLESS

## Why go out hunting when you can make your food come to you?

The **walking flower mantis**, disguised as a beautiful orchid, sits and waits for its dinner to arrive. When butterflies, bees, or grasshoppers come looking for pollen or nectar to eat, the mantis snaps them up in its trap-like front legs. Instead of finding a meal, these visiting insects end up as a tasty meal themselves. Then the mantis goes back to looking like just another harmless flower . . .

Forest quaker

Tiny grass blue

Who, me? I'm just a flower!

# BITE!

Immensely powerful jaws are a good thing to have as a predator. With a fast, strong bite, these hunters take down big prey.

## Loaded lip

**Dragonfly nymphs** grow up underwater. They hide in the pebbles and plants at the bottom of the pond. When a tasty fish or frog swims by, they don't have to jump out to catch it because they wear a spear gun on their face. They shoot out a special lip that's half as long as their body to grab it and bring it back to their mouth. It shoots out too fast to see, in just a few milliseconds. The prey don't know what hit them.

Tadpoles

Common minnow

30

## Turn the tables

Usually, frogs eat beetles. Frogs are bigger than beetles, and they have speedy, sticky tongues. But when a frog tries to eat an *Epomis ground beetle*, the beetle eats the frog instead. Sometimes the frog swallows them first—but then it spits them back out. The beetle jumps on the frog's back, slices through its spine with one bite, and has dinner.

Savigny's treefrog

Ground beetles are so tough, even babies take on frogs.

# AMAZING WAYS TO HUNT

**Jumping spiders** are the tigers of the spider world. With their four forward-facing eyes, they have much better eyesight than almost any bug. They can also jump over 30 times their body length. They don't spin webs—they stalk their prey, leap on it, and paralyze it with their bite. Silk is just a safety line for them.

*Fruit fly*

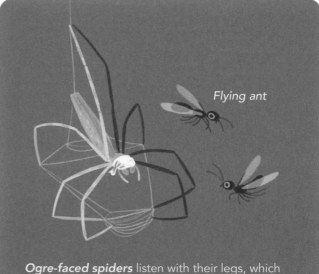

*Flying ant*

**Ogre-faced spiders** listen with their legs, which have special vibration-sensing organs. They hang upside down in their webs, and when they hear prey, they do a backflip and catch it in a small silk net they've been holding. They can even do it blindfolded (yes, scientists make tiny blindfolds for spiders).

*Green bottle fly*

**Turret spiders** hide inside silk-lined towers. They build them out of mud, moss, and leaves, then line them with soft white silk. When they feel the footsteps of passing prey, they launch a sneak attack from their tiny forest castle.

**Bolas spiders** hunt with a sticky yo-yo, a silk thread with a drop of glue on the end. They hunt moths. At night. While hanging upside down. They produce a scent that the moths can't resist. Sensitive hairs on their legs warn them when a moth is approaching. *Whap!* They swing out their sticky yo-yo, hit the moth as it flies by in the dark, and pull in their prey for a deadly bite.

*Lydia lichen moth*

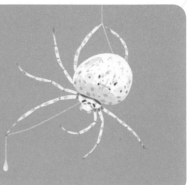

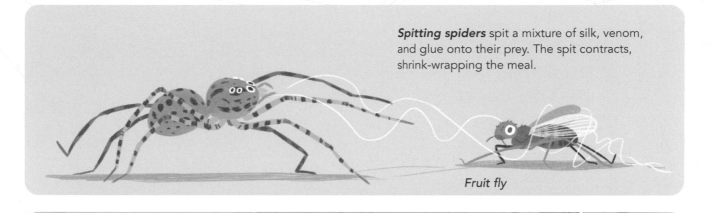

**Spitting spiders** spit a mixture of silk, venom, and glue onto their prey. The spit contracts, shrink-wrapping the meal.

Fruit fly

**Fishing spiders** can walk on water. They hunt along stream and pond banks by sensing vibrations caused by fallen insects or small fish and tadpoles.

Tadpole

**Cribellate spiders** make sticky webs without using glue like most spiders do. Cribellate webs are made of fuzzy silk that is sticky like Velcro. The spiders spin many ultrafine strands, then use a special comb on their back legs to fuzz it up.

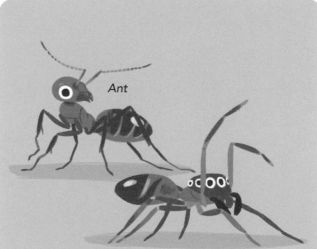

Ant

**Ant mimic spiders** look just like ants—so they can hunt ants. They wave their front legs to look like antennae and they copy the ants' way of walking. They hunt only the ants they look like.

# BETTER BUDDY UP

Tiny creatures might seem like the ones that need protection from bigger creatures. But sometimes they are the ones who protect bigger creatures! Some microbes wrap their host in an invisibility cloak made of moonbeams. Armies of ants protect trees from huge herbivores. Herds of honeydew-producing bugs feed whole colonies of ants. And sometimes, the smaller creature just takes a free ride.

The **golden medusa jellyfish** has algae living in its tissues that convert the sun's energy into food that they share with the jellyfish. The jellyfish gets most of its food from the algae.

# INVISI-SQUID

About the size of a walnut, the *Hawaiian bobtail squid* would make a great snack for many ocean creatures. In the daytime, it stays hidden in the sand. But at night, it has to swim up near the surface to hunt. It has a flashlight that helps it hide.

_Bluestripe snapper_

When the bobtail squid swims up from the sandy ocean bottom, it shines light below, matching the moonlight shimmering through the waves above, so predators can't see its shadow. The light comes from glowing bacteria it keeps in its belly.

The bacteria living in the squid's belly benefit, too. They get to live safe inside the squid. The squid gives them food and oxygen. In return, the bacteria wrap an invisibility cloak around the squid while it's hunting.

# PROTECTION

It's not just tiny creatures who need protection. Sometimes big creatures need help, too. And sometimes smaller creatures are the ones who help them by sharing their superpowers.

## Ants versus elephants

*Elephants* roam the plains of Kenya, and they like to eat acacia trees. To avoid being destroyed by their tearing trunks, the **whistling thorn acacia** has made powerful friends: **ants**. These tiny bodyguards protect these trees against the largest herbivore on the planet. The acacia's branches are covered in thorns with round hollow bases, about the size of a ping-pong ball. Ants bore holes in the thorn bases and make them into cozy homes. The acacia also feeds the ants drops of sweet nectar, made by special glands near the leaves. In return, the ants defend the tree. When an elephant wraps its trunk around a branch, a swarm of ants attacks, biting the inside of the elephant's nose! The elephant quickly learns not to eat whistling thorn acacias.

The holes in the hollow thorns make them whistle when the wind blows.

## Punch with pom-poms

**Boxer crabs** carry an **anemone** in each claw. The anemones are armed with nematocysts, tiny toxin-tipped harpoons, so any attacker gets a stinging surprise. With these deadly pom-poms, tiny boxer crabs can fend off bigger predators with powerful punches. The anemones in their claws deliver a painful sting. Boxer crabs also use the anemones in their claws to gather food, waving them around to sting small creatures, then bringing the food-loaded gloves to their mouths to feed. The crabs control how much the anemones eat, keeping them small on purpose, so they don't get too big to carry.

*Sergeant major damselfish*

If a boxer crab loses its anemones, it doesn't use its anemone claws until it can attack another boxer crab and steal an anemone.

# WHY HUNT WHEN YOU CAN HERD?

**Some creatures grow their own food right at home, so they don't have to go hunting.**

## Honeydew herders

Like people keep cows, some *ants* tend herds of *aphids*, little bugs that drink plant sap and squirt out sweet honeydew. To ask for honeydew to drink, the ants stroke the aphids with their antennae, then catch the drop of sugary liquid, a lot like milking a cow. In return, the ants protect the aphids from their predators, like ladybugs, and carry them to parts of the plant with sweeter sap, like cowherds take their herds to greener pastures.

*Ladybug*

Cows can't fly, so fences are enough to stop them from wandering off. But aphids can grow wings. So the ants bite off the aphids' wings, ouch! They also spread chemicals that slow the aphids down, like aphid tranquilizers, keeping them calm and close by. When ants form a new colony, they take some aphids with them.

## Grow a garden in your fur

**Sloths** live in trees, and they move so slowly that their name in Spanish is los perezosos which means "the lazies." They can't afford to move fast, because they only eat leaves, and they don't get much energy from them. For extra food, sloths grow **algae** gardens in their fur and then nibble it for more nutrients. Sloth fur is full of cracks and it holds water like a sponge, making it a nice place for algae to live. The algae in sloth fur isn't found anywhere else and moms pass it to their babies when they are only a few weeks old. The algae need fertilizer to grow well, so the sloths keep moths in their fur. The moth poop is like compost for the algae gardens.

Snout moth

As a bonus, the algae turns the sloths green, giving them a bit of camouflage.

# JUST OUT FOR A JOYRIDE

**Shrimpy shrimp stay safe by hitching a ride on a poisonous magic carpet.**

*Imperial shrimp* are small, and they don't like to swim around the ocean on their own. They ride on the backs of **nudibranchs**, like magic carpets. The imperial shrimp only pairs up with a few kinds of large, colorful nudibranchs. The nudibranchs are toxic to eat, so most predators avoid them. Since the shrimp are just riding along, the poison's no problem for them, and they get protection from predators. The nudibranchs roam in search of food. When its mount stops to feed, the shrimp leans over the side to collect its own meal.

*Gem nudibranch*

It's not clear if imperial shrimp help the nudibranchs they ride. They might do a bit of tidying up, but they might not. Nudibranchs without shrimp are just fine, but the shrimp are never found without a mount. These shrimp might just be taking a free ride.

# MAYBE IT'S NOT SO TOUGH TO BE TINY AFTER ALL!

Tiny creatures are tougher than they seem. From glitter disguises to poo umbrellas, they have amazing ways to defend themselves. Tiny hunters carry weapons like sticky yo-yos and harpoon teeth that are as strong as they are small. And tiny partners help out larger ones in some very big ways.